shaking off the ashes

59 poems of phoenix rising moments

curated & introduced by melanie sue hicks

edited by sarah hanson

Inked Elephant Publishing House, LLC
A Social Impact Publisher

LIBRARY OF CONGRESS CATALOGUING-IN-PUBLICATION NAMES: Melanie Sue Hicks

TITLE: Shaking Off the Ashes, Poems of Phoenix Rising Moments

DESCRIPTION: Castle Rock: Inked Elephant Publishing House, 2024

IDENTIFIERS: ISBN 978-1-959694-13-7

LIBRARY OF CONGRESS CONTROL NUMBER: 2024949572

BISAC: Poetry / Women Authors

DESIGN AND COMPOSITION: Neon Pig Creative

COVER DESIGN: Neon Pig Creative

COVER IMAGES: krustovin / AdobeStock #358901123

TYPOGRAPHY: Flamenco, designed by LatinoType
Kopius, designed by Sibylle Hagmann from Kontour
Mr. Eaves, designed by Zuzana Licko from Emigre

Printed in the United States of America.

Some names and identifying characteristics have been changed to protect the privacy of the individuals involved.

Inked Elephant Publishing House is committed to amplifying the works of quality and authenticity. In that spirit, we are proud to offer this book to our readers, however, the story, experiences, and words are the author's alone.

let

me

begin

again

-philip levin

introduction

becoming aspens

The year 2023 held both the highest and lowest points of my life. The publication of my long-awaited first book followed directly by a layoff from both my job and my marriage, within weeks of one another. The duality of this contrasting life reality left me flailing. Sleepless nights questioning everything. The film reel of my life to-date playing on repeat while I meticulously scrutinized my behaviors, my words, my intentions. Blessed with friends and family who would help if they knew how, I attempted to cope in the way I had always coped...alone.

Then I boarded a plane bound for Italy, and unknowingly changed my life forever. There, in the rolling hills of a vineyard, under the famous Tuscan sky, we found each other. Strangers who became intertwined like the roots of an Aspen, unclear where one ends and another begins.

We came from across the US and abroad, each pulling a heavy wagon of boxes from our mind's attic. Boxes of joy, boxes of pain, boxes of hope, boxes of despair. We piled them all in the middle of a room surrounded by yoga mats and journals and carefully sorted them into piles of what to honor and what to discard.

We held each other, literally and metaphorically, through the misery of pain and the triumph of uncomfortable growth. Day by day we laid bricks of trust that became a foundation, a lifeboat in the swell of life's dark ocean. We sat emotionally naked, exposing our cracked imperfections and collectively poured gold to bond us into a single kintsugi bowl.

When the week concluded, we embraced through tears that lasted longer than the norm and yet never long enough. We scattered back across the world to our respective corners, somehow tethered together by an invisible thread. A thread that might go silent but can never truly be severed.

these are the stories

These stories represent the fabric of intertwined life that we brought to Tuscany and quilted together through poetry. Some written there, some just seeds planted there. In what follows, we share pieces of ourselves at various stages of life and growth.

They are organized in four parts, a symbolic representation of the spherical nature of healing.

SECTION 1 **Burn it All Down.** We unapologetically share our rage – at others, at life, at ourselves. Sometimes life is simply in too much disarray to do anything except burn it all down and start anew.

SECTION 2 **Tears From Heaven.** This is a reflection on grief. As we sit among ashes, covered in soot and char, we grieve what once was. Or perhaps our grief is the realization that our perception was not reality.

SECTION 3 **Stand Among Flames.** Words to remind us that, from the depths of despair, we can always muster the strength to rise, even just to our knees.

SECTION 4 **The View From Above.** Words of reclamation. Only after we have been through the fire, can we regrow our wings. Only with new wings, can we begin to truly soar.

It is with great appreciation to my Tuscan beauties for giving so authentically to this work. We hope you, dear reader, can ride the wave of human emotion with us and by the end, triumphantly shake off the ashes of your own life and rise again.

ALL MY LOVE,

Melanie Sue Hicks

1 burn it all down

2 tears from heaven

3 stand among flames

4 the view from above

1

burn it all down

POEMS OF ANGER AND RAGE

noon

I could smell the pig shit.

It was caked in the creases of his coveralls as he burst through the door.

The heat and humidity of the Indiana summer hung heavily on him,

penetrating the kitchen where my mother and I were eating our tuna salad sandwiches.

It was noon.

He only had half an hour for lunch

and he devoured us all.

I watched him as he sat down

across the speckled Formica table from me

and shoved fistfuls of Doritos

then tuna salad into his mouth.

Orange and tan clumps of spittle collected in his beard

as he slopped up everything my mother placed before him at his trough.

Tuna and mayonnaise don't mix well with pig shit in a house without air conditioning in July.

My own mouth was caked with wet and gummy balls of Wonder Bread

that I forcefully swallowed and willed to go down my throat.

I imagined myself more invisible with every bite.

I was always choking when he was around.

My eyes began to burn.

There was never enough air,

not when he smelled like pig shit or weed or beer;

not when he stuck his hands down my shorts that same summer,

and not afterwards when he beat the ever-loving shit out of my mother.

BY KRIS LINGENFELTER

sleight of hand

Sleight of hand
mentalist man
made an x appear
on the palm my closed fist
my stomach flipped at the sight
chills ran up my arms
       he never touched
he said *they never feel it*
       he never touched
only no one believed it
they all thought I missed it
he must have touched
I started doubting myself
       did he?
       touch me?
was this *less* trick
more joke
on me
that happens
doubting
distrusting
always ready to play back up
following me onto the stage
the bit wasn't through
my ring became the disappearing act
he motioned to my ring
called to my husband seated recording
"nice work"

then a flourish of his hands
outlining
my thick curvaceous body
in thin air
repeating with more gusto and a wink
"NICE WORK"
as if I had been formed
BY my husbands hands or FOR his hands alone
I blushed at the compliment
even with the heavy pour of misogyny
truth is
I felt pretty that night
my favorite green dress
and sparkly necklace
I felt pretty
until
I watched it back
WAIT
"nice work" was a joke
mocking me
or
my eyes deceiving me
or not
funhouse mirror
dysmorphic distortion
disguised words
with too white teeth
so sharp
I didn't bleed
until I saw for myself
they never feel it

he did say
slight of hand
magic man
the whole time
I swear he never touched me
nevertheless
the trick
illusion of pretty
like the x
the trick
revealed
the fool
was me

BY FAITH SCOTT

independent of

you

Sometimes I get an urge
to smash a life right
in your face.

Shove
the things I've done for our family -
independent of you -
into your nose.
But,
that'd be separating
what got created inside of our union
and
I can't.

So I'll stand here until the wave of anger passes,
let the weight of the world
lift and carry on.
I wish you were aware
of it all,
but
maybe that's how you survive it yourself,
being away.

Mentally and physically...
but
I know you're mentally there,
just shutting down that you care.

It makes me sad -
but
maybe that's my
weight of the world.
Caring.

eau du bravery

The "How-dare-she" whispers
follow my bravest choices
like a perfume cloud,

heavy with the expectation
that I evaporate myself back into
the ether of their approval.

I let my courage linger in the air
for them to choke on.

who are you to presume?.

Just a few moments of down
time: opening Instagram, a fatal
mistake. Amidst likes and hearts, between
words of encouragement,
a comment. Daggers of righteous

condemnation meant to strike
and kill, admonishing me, raising him
to icon status. I would be sorry I left.
I left... As if I was the one to leave.
Instantly that tufted brown couch

became a vessel for my hysterics
This trip. Booked through tear-soaked
eyes, mascara running onto the keyboard,
swept up the pieces of my shredded
soul, packed in a suitcase and eight

hours numb on a plane. This trip.
The one I begged God to allow the Tuscan
sun to cobble this heart back together
so I could ever love again, live again. This trip.
A gift I gave myself to run from all reminders

of him, from the vast cavern of loneliness
in my soul echoing in the empty right side
of our bed. To forget, for just a moment,
the sound of his laugh, the feel of his hands,
the look in his eyes when he still loved me.

Photos on Instagram show laughter and smiles
because we don't take pictures of hours
spent swimming in oceans of shed tears.
Photos on Instagram depict joy and friendship
because we don't hold phones when we are holding

each other while rocking back and forth
through howls of weeping. Photos on Instagram
pay homage to sunshine and historic vistas
because we use these as backdrops as we try
to make sense of life's cruelties. And just

when these careless words could have accomplished
their mission, crushed me into the magma
of earth's center never to join reality again,
they showed up. Descending like the Persian
Army in the Battle of Thermopylae. Grabbing

my phone, deleting hateful words from the ether,
preventing me from drowning as my heart gasped
for air. Taking me into their arms, reminding
me I am loved. Not a moment lost.
Doing anything they could to repair

what they did not break. So, I say to you, sir:
Who are you to presume you know
my story? Who are you to presume you know
the truth, held within the four walls of what was once
our home? Who are you to add to the weight

on my shattered heart? Find someone else
to demean with your ignorant words. I have a fierce
squad of protectors who know truth
and see promise and will die on your sword
before they let you stab me further

This is what love looks like.

BY MELANIE SUE HICKS

what now

The rug pulled out
And yet my world remained. What was significant
Now trivial.
Who cares what they think
When little eyes are watching
The show and telling.
What really matters
After the curtain is drawn back.
The living can choose
Agency
Or complacency
The decisions we don't make
Are made
Inertia a fearsome adversary
Fulfilling our prophecies
With blame to spare.
We can see in others
What we can't in ourselves
Saying it enough times doesn't make it true
Avoid until avoidance is the story
Or until the excuses catch in your throat
Dry heaves of empty words.
Breathe
Rip the Band-Aid off
Leave the guardrails behind
Be and listen.
The heart hears in the quiet
Recognizes real
Knows truth.
Move forward
A step is a choice.

BY DEBORAH CAMPBELL

a sense of self

BY MAURA McLAUGHLIN

I feel stupid and small and foolish and weak
I followed a bird's note and I'm on the street
Alone with proverbial egg on my face
Feeling the wake of my own fall from grace
Get up you stupid - it's your own damn fault
A road that you trusted like a heavenly Gestalt
Get a grip, get a sense of yourself
Let the feelings ferment, let the sweetness turn sour
So you can live on - present hour by hour
The future is over, the present is the same

The one that you honor holds on to a different name
Get a grip, get a sense of yourself
Get out of this picture - put that dream on the shelf

medusa mother

with soft wide teeth
she will bear down
crackling into crumbled shards
opaque and silver
sometimes choking
she does her best
to cough up and chew down
bitter cud of nothingness
suddenly sweet
but then always stings
her raspberry lips
standing guard as leather strap
clenching hard
with each pang
labor had begun and did continue
although there was no sign of dilation
only the pressure to push
her spine rejecting numbing needle
she held as still as she could
but she just kept flinching
she just kept swelling
she just kept aching
unsteady though standing
they try to feed her
hold her head above her listless heart
squatting low in ritualistic posture
atop red bricks
expelling steam
strength-giving fennel
bearing down once more

then again and again
finally going limp
yet does not pass
only resting lightly
on her knees
praying posture
inhaling hopped perseverance
to endure
they keep watching
stand waiting
dark corners
going about the business of their days
listening carefully for a cry of new life
but hear none
only unrelenting bellows
childless lament
some can no longer bear
some even distrust
she could not simply choose
to stand upright once again
warrior slant restored
still afraid to touch
or be touched
phantom breech birth
some can no longer look
Medusa Mother
it may spread onto them
staining them like blood
relentless
gaseous and palpable
most unprolific affliction
they do not know of such things
nor want to

BY FAITH SCOTT

against my own will

When did it start and when does it end?
It starts with force, no sign of a friend.
It ends after chaos, the life in between.
A freak out, a piercing, a girl becomes mean.
It looks to the world that she's become one of those.
A person with multiple holes in her nose.
Because somewhere deep down she wrongly holds shame.
Like a question or a hint of some source of blame.
Did she bring this on?
Create a bad dream?
Hold her own head down to muffle a scream?
Fuck that, no she didn't, and fuck you for believing,
That we bring this stuff on, no reason for grieving.
Consider instead that she said yes to this life,
To become a woman who lives without strife.

Taking on bullies from both sides of the field,
the wounded, the broken, the ones with a shield.
Stand back she might say, for I have been raped.
I now behave rabid like a wolf who's been caped.
If you try to contain my rage, against my own will,
I recommend that you don't... stand back and hold still.
That's when it ends, the effect that it has,
Until then, if you cross her, she will kick your ass.

BY MAURA McLAUGHLIN

2

tears from heaven

POEMS OF SADNESS AND GRIEF

grief season

Astrologists say Cancer season lasts four
weeks in the middle of summer. Yours lasted
eight harvests; your tumor sprouted in the high
heat of my tenth birthday and grew all

through the winter of my eighteenth year.
After the reaping on that January hospital day,
Fallow season fell and fell and fell; my sorrow
a snowstorm that lasted two decades.

To lose a parent young
is to spend years asking their memory:
Do you remember me?
Are you proud of me?

Is this good? Am I good?

And you, a man of few words in life,
respond just as quietly after your death.
It has taken me these last twenty years
without you, to learn to listen:

a slight breeze across my face, soft
as the shearling collar and worn elbows of
your favorite leather jacket, still holding
the memory of your aftershave for me to breathe in,

and a whisper so faint that the hairs on my
arms can hear you only when they stand
upright at full attention, tall as the
sweetcorn fields where you would let

me pretend to get lost amid
the stalks that also stood twice my height -
"Yes, Sarah. Yes. I never lost
sight of you, not even once."

I rub my hands over my forearms,
and walk on into the next 20 years:

Healing season now.

BY SARAH HANSON

love child

Sounds magical
Enchanted tale
happily, ever after
except it wasn't
more like
drafted
upon arrival
dog tags around my neck
did not belong on a baby
named Faith for my
call of duty
really
for me to bring them
together
so sweet
but not
and yet, that's how the story goes
they'd say
See
Look
We have faith
Look
Right there
She is ours
The only ours
Not yours
or mine
but ours
dibs
The only ours
We can claim

And

will

we

ever

The only ours

We can all

Point to

Resent

Blame

Torment

Sorryimsorryimsorryyourerightimwrongthatneverhappened

We have

faith took the fall

took the blame

faith can take it

faith takes everything

So of course

faith fell

       short

           and shorter

even as she grew

           taller and fuller

                    shinier and brighter

Imsorryagainitwasmyfaultiwastoofullofmyselfyourerightimwrong

       even though she never saw it

                never ever felt it

in their reflections

       mirrors always distorted

           light and shadow tricks

               only the terrors and horrors

                   she committed

• • •

by daring to be

                                b

                                o

                                r

                                n

            ours

            ours

            ours

they did not take it well

            so faith took more

before she could ride her banana seat

            reading rooms

                        was a magic trick

faith would be sure of what

            T H E Y

            hoped for

            and certain of what

            they damn well better see

                        gulps of their pain

                        bitterness stuck in her teeth

                        burning down her throat

faith sure as hell better not forget

            what she was never there to cause

doesn't matter

            she should have known better

            she had two parents

everything

            T H E Y

            did not

always sick from the thickness
      monsters under their beds and in their dreams
        found their way to her room at night
    down the hall
       she was just sleeping
         fresh meat to feast
s i l e n c e
nightmares yet to be shaken
heartache demons
maybe they were sleepwalking
you can't wake them
    do
    not
    wake
    them
how
could
    a l l   t h i s
       be my fault
imissedityourerightialwaysdothatwrong
the paint of the new scenery
still wet
sliding down the wall where glasses
were thrown
    we don't talk about that
refrigerator door broken
    from a body getting shoved against
toughen up
    I hate being tickled
      It's not funny
      It hurts
       Stop

•
•
•

. . .

I peed my pants
        Because
        you wouldn't stop
we don't talk about that
what'd you say to me
shut your mouth
don't eat that
you are not special
spoiled
you don't know anything
naïve
you're selfish
brat
But you better fucking shine
remember you are OURS
and don't you ever dare say,

"But I am MINE."

the gap

BY MAURA McLAUGHLIN

SHAKING OFF THE ASHES

I want to lay my hands on you.

I want to heal my false bravado by loving you.

You have the best of me and I don't know if

you want it and I don't know how to not care if you don't.

the coat

Depression hangs
from my shoulders, melancholy cloaking
my body in worry and sadness, an old,
familiar wool coat. My body is compressed
with the heaviness of its utility. Some of the

threads have unraveled from the buttons
and along the collar, filamentous fibers
like glass shards that deftly scratch and slice
my neck. The coat is a gift from my mother,
given to her by my grandmother and my great-

grandmother before her. It is a hand-me-down
from my father, a remnant from "the good old days."
I was born to wear this coat. I can't help but
wear it. It has taken on the shape of my body
and I have grown accustomed to its weight.

I am who I am because this coat has defined me.
I don't know how to get through a winter
without it and there are times when I am afraid

that it will always be winter. Sometimes I surprise
myself and get a glimpse of springtime.

I take off the coat and hang it up or leave it
on a chair. I marvel at my freedom and wonder
why I let it take up so much space in my closet.
I tell myself that the next year won't be as cold;
that it might be good to try a lighter coat, maybe

something a little brighter with some colors
woven into a new fabric. It feels good to look
in the mirror and see myself uncloaked.
It feels good to notice the springtime.
Then I realize one of my kids has found the coat

where I had left it and has put it on. I watch
helplessly as they fasten the buttons, tug
at the sleeves, and pull the collar up high around
their neck, waiting for the chill they know is coming.
Their hands feel along the sides of the coat,

obsessing over every small detail in the weave.
Their mind catalogs every loose strand,
and they admonish themselves over their own
unraveling. I always beg them to take off the coat.
My desperation only makes them disappear

further into it, their bodies wrapped in our shared
tapestry. Even if I steal it back, they'll just

find it again. Like me, they just can't help themselves.

BY KRIS LINGENFELTER

ways he broke me

Don't show
emotion, he can't
hold it.
Don't cry, he will
never
comfort you.
Don't ask for
resolution, he won't
give it.
Don't crack
jokes, there is
no room for play.
Don't get
upset, it's not
a big deal.
Don't have
a moment of
insecurity, show
no weakness.
Take lashes spewed
in drunken words:
piece of shit,
annoying,
I'll never
love you.
How long
do I allow this?
Why do I
allow it at all?

BY MELANIE SUE HICKS

I'm having a pity party
Only I'm invited
I don't want you to come
I'm the guest of honor
You can't share my spotlight
It's my time, all mine

BY LEE TYRELL BARRON

leave me

alone

combat boots to a funeral

Eighteen hours before my stepfather took his
last breath, tucked under the thinnest scratch
of the hospital blanket and braced against the
tumor filling his lungs, I was wrapping myself in

winter flannel to brace against January
winds and the chill of being the saddest kid at the mall.
The air was rich with the salted dough of kiosk
pretzels, but my nose was thick with the antiseptic we'd

been breathing for weeks as we counted to these final
days. I bought a new pair of Doc Marten boots that
night,
black and combative as my eighteen-year-old angst.
There
was nothing wrong with the pair I already owned, except

that they had walked that waxed hospital linoleum all
winter and I couldn't bear to have them on my feet one
minute longer. Sitting on the edge of his bed the next
morning, our tears the only thing softening that horrid

blanket fabric and my feet blistering from the painful
chafe of new stiff leather, I held my hand over his
cold, skeletal fingers and told him every goodbye
word, whole chapters pouring forth, afraid to stop lest

I miss something important. He gave a ghost
of a squeeze and whispered "Sarah, I loved you like
you were my own daughter." He died thirty minutes later.
I wore my new boots to his funeral, and my feet ached

every fucking minute of the entire ceremony.

the weight of hate

He left an unseen scar,
betrayal and the death of hope.

My dream life, dream
house, dream love,

cleaved inside the rearview
of his departure.

I was left in wreckage.

My heart broke again
at my father's crumpled face,

who had opened his family to a protector,
believed he would love his daughter.

He lied to my father's open heart.

My father's tears,
my sobs, his disbelief,

a paternal phone call, trying
to convince him to stay.

How could he leave?

If our hatred has atomic mass,
it only weighs on the ones who stay.

It is impossible not to be changed
by the heaviness.

BY MELANIE SUE HICKS

hero of the m25

Morning after morning, as I slowly
rolled by in my viewing box I observed

you on the temporary construction wall
of the M25, lying in state. Did a road

worker gently place you there, sensing
your regalness? Did he witness your fall?

Perhaps your last battle against the lorries.
For several months you stood against

sun and rain, wind and even snow.

In death you proved how resilient you were,
how proud Your life's challenges won.

Peace and rest
yours now forever.

Crow or raven,
my hero.

BY LEE TYRELL BARRON

safe space

I called you my best
friend, I called you my safe
space. How wrong I was.

The miles of shoreline we walked,
foreign lands explored, elephants
rode, mountains climbed.

The tears we wiped, joys applauded,
dreams fostered, years shared.
The tequila shots in Mexico.

We told of our marriages,
yours and mine. I never thought
to use your words as a weapon.

That's how we differ I guess.

I left the neighborhood.
Unbeknownst to me,
I also left your heart.

I will miss you, maybe
forever. An ended friendship
feels like a death, and yet you still live.

losing them–finding HIM

No amount of power from these engines can lift my heart off the
ground
We are 20,000 feet up in the sky
Yet my heart is still being dragged
Anchored to the ground

It is dragged behind me most days.
sometimes I am walking backwards trying to pull it along
all the while torn by the cobblestone streets you left me in

On my better days, my friends and loved ones carry it for me.
Too heavy for some to bear alone,
but together they lift it slightly and bandage what they can.
Enough to get me going.

When they put it down, it is once again dragged
Through rough roads, dirt and weeds.

There is a huge hole where you all once were before you were taken.
Pulled in the direction that looked good
But entirely the wrong way.
You were told it was a one way street.
But that isn't true.

You were told lies to keep you going the wrong way.
Promised a better life than what we gave.
Lies only to be left hanging by a thin wire.
A wire too thick to cut that started wrapping around you tight

Until you couldn't breathe.
Until you couldn't see.

All the while, the whispers in your ears telling you
that you needed the wire for protection.
Telling you to trust it.
Telling you that this was best

I scream for you but you cannot hear me.
There is too much noise in your ears.
The whispers are so plentiful
Louder than any screams.
You are spinning in circles and cannot stop.
I try to stop the storm you have become
But I am only one
I am no match for the storm alone.

Your babies need your attention.
You must give yourself to them.
The energy you have left, which isn't much.
They need all you have.

.
.
.

. . .

I reach out for you but you are too far.
I seem to get very close.
My fingers brush yours but then you are too far again.
So close.
Then the storm becomes very fierce
Blowing hard and sweeping you away as dust.

I scream as my voice becomes weak.
My whole self becomes weak and my knees buckle.
My body feels numb.
I feel like I am looking at myself from above.
Like my soul is watching as I lose strength.
As I die slowly.

It used to seem easy to breathe.
Not anymore
It's not automatic as it always seems to be.
My breathing shallows
I keep telling myself I need to breathe deeper and longer.
Sometimes it stops completely and then I gasp
A reminder to keep breathing.
If I really stop breathing would the pain also stop.

I think of the others who love me.
I pray.
I pray for the God, that I hope is there
To help me breathe.
I pray that He helps me get up and carry my legs, my head, my heart, my whole self.
I pray for him to help me stay alive.
And then I do it all again the next day.
And the next.
And I have learned one thing; that God is real.

So I will pray for strength to keep carrying on in this life.
I may have to drag this heart of mine behind me for the rest of my days,
I pray to thank Him for giving me the strength to help myself
I pray for the beautiful loved ones I have met in this life,
I may have lost some for now, but I found Him.

BY JENNIFER BRYANT

another version of our story

In another version, I lie
in bed tracing your tattoos
with my fingertips.
I nestle into your spoon at dawn

instead of wiggling away,
pups sleep in their own beds,
no chasm formed between us.

I rise with you early and rest
my head on your shoulder
over coffee. We turn off
the tv, dance in our kitchen,

make pasta together.
I tell you daily what you mean
to me, double down on vulnerability

not independence. I rise early
take in sunrises on the boat.
In another version,
you do not wear disappointment.

We plan date nights, you reach
for my hand to hold.
You never move

to the bed downstairs.
Your face lights at the sight of me
In another version we live happily,
you still love me.

You do not fall in love with another,
there is no goodbye.
And yet,
                                 there is no other version.

buddha belly baby girl

Buddha Belly Baby Girl
kool-aid smile
no thought to my buddha
No worries
just glee
Joy pure
Feeling the sunshine
warm on my skin
orange and glowy
behind my eyelids
felt good
that's all
just
good
peaceful
unfettered
My heart aches now to see
Mickey Mouse terry cloth towel
spread out on the cool, cool grass
smooth and a little slick still
from last night's sprinklers
baby oil slathered across
my sister's perfectly brown body
just outside the frame
crisco was the secret ingredient
mixed in with cocoa butter
I can still smell it
slow-cooking
requires patience
like making pancakes

cook on low heat
wait for the bubbles to pop
you have to wait
I had a hard time waiting
Still
The flip was always a disaster
Still
I always try to smooth out and pat down
like the teenage couple
sitting on the old squishy coffee house couch
lumpy-sunken in the middle
first date
no firmness
all awkward stiffness
he slouched in
making a "c" shape
lower case
that is certain
hunching toward her
she stiffened

• • •

• • •

making her back a capital "S"
cut off at the top
She had one arm across her lap like a safety bar on a roller coaster
She never wanted to get on this ride
her friend talked her into it
She could close her eyes if it got too scary
She chewed her gum nervously
a little like cud
I do this too
She kept pulling at her hair with the other hand
Her fingers twisting and untwisting
around and around dark curly strands
drawing away a few pieces each time
subtle, but I know the trick
I saw the miniscule hair hill forming on the tile by her raspberry
chucks.
He didn't notice
(They really don't notice)
His eyes never left the peep show of her too snug top she borrowed
from her friend
(some fucking friend)
that showed her curves
gaping open between the buttons
boys love that
she hated it
more twists and untwists and plucks
tiny hair hill grows
the door pushed open too wide
jingling loudly
a 4 year old girl in kitten rain boots with a sparkly tutu
cape with a lightning bolt
and a foam sword blew in

I saw her sweet belly happily spill over the waist of red leggings with
purple stars and the tutu so she could breathe and laugh and giggle
I wondered if the teenage girl
could breathe enough
I remembered my sister blowing purple bubbles with her gum that
day in the sun and a mean boy coming up to flirt with her
he asked me if I swallowed a basketball
I remember the pop of the bubble
and dropping my head
to see it and feel wrong
for the first time
the giggles and snickers told me
I wasn't at all like her
my baby buddha belly
was no longer happy
just then
that moment
that was it
with the sudden jingling
the coffee house door opening again
I glanced back and the teenage couple was walking out
I felt sadness for her
wondering what was left on the rollercoaster ride
or at the amusement park
I frantically looked back down
for the hair hill
she had made next to her
raspberry chucks
but it had already blown away like tumbleweed in a ghost town

BY FAITH SCOTT

SHAKING OFF THE ASHES

3

stand among flames

POEMS OF STRENGTH AND RESILIENCE

inner asshole

What to do when your inner asshole won't go away
Stop
Close your eyes
take a long, slow, deep breath
In through your nose
Like inhaling the magic of the salt water fragrance of the ocean
Hold it for a couple beats
Then blow slowly out through your mouth
Like blowing a dandelion puff after a wish is made
Then, open your eyes and look that asshole STRAIGHT ON,
like the badass you desire to be (and actually already are)
You just might see that she is not all that scary actually she is so
afraid
So fucking fearful
certain that everything will fall apart
Cynicism and criticism are so much easier
Than hope and curiosity and wonder
She may not/probably won't even be able to look back at you in
the eye
Or perhaps
her venom will get hotter and stronger

Either way
Hold your gaze
Steel your spine
She is fighting you
She is fighting you
Because she IS you
She is the YOU that was terrified in 7th grade with stained pants
because pads are so stupid and your Mama thought tampons
meant you were loose...like, HUH?!
And someone mercilessly grabbed the hoodie wrapped tightly
around your waist
in the cafeteria
Goddammit
Everyone saw and so the asshole voice got louder
"Don't ever forget THAT"
She is the YOU that awkwardly stood in department store mirrors in
clothes that were too small because you were told
THIS was the size she should be
so you better remember
the pinching and discomfort and mortifyingly
hot shame
the next time you want to eat chips or chocolate
"You better remember that"
She is the you that got broken on a bed at 19
by a stupid boy who lied a lot and convinced you
you made it happen
because you started it
he can't control how you make him feel
he loved you so much it hurt
it hurt

• • •

"you have to remember, love hurts"
She is the you that couldn't keep a pregnancy,
no matter how many times you tried
how many ways you tried
all the prayers and books and advice from
well-meaning assholes
no matter how many specialists and therapists
pills and shots
tests and numbers
calls and blood, always blood
sonograms and more sonograms
and all the pregnant women waiting to go back and get the
printed proof of their completeness
their womanhood

all the phone calls from friends crying awkward apologies and
forewarning the night prior to announcing they're expecting
Never having to guess who
because I already knew
And the expecting
all the fucking expecting
expectations and baby showers
that would sting like lightning strikes
guttural cries
desperation on the bathroom floor
more than one bathroom floor
She is that you
"Godammit DO NOT FORGET THAT"
She is 13 and 16 and 19 and twentysomething and like 36, with a
fucking hysterectomy scar, and just yesterday, at almost 50 even
She wasn't always an asshole
The louder she gets, the more afraid she is
She is just so fucking hurt and jaded
And scared and wants to protect
Just can't bear to let you hope
But YOU can...
She wasn't always an asshole
and beloved,
neither
are
you

BY FAITH SCOTT

the lioness

On a bridge
The dam breaks
Tears flow
How apropos
This cosmic irony.
Fireworks he called it
A system in overdrive
Overkill, attacking itself
Attacking her
My glorious Amazon.
Standing on tippy toes
I reach up
Enveloping her
I am big
I am strong
I will keep you safe
We believe me
We want to believe me.
Cupping water in my hands
Splashing my face
The water trickles down
A white flash
Stark against dark hair
Barely dusted by salt.

BY DEBORAH CAMPBELL

I look into my eyes
Fear looks back
Please let her be okay
Please let her be okay
The new mantra.
A white flash
My kryptonite.
It screams at me
In every reflection.
Rumblings grow
I roar back Finally.
Fear does not heal.
Cupping water in my hands
Splashing my face
The water trickles down
Bright and shorn
I look into my eyes
A lioness gazes back.
She is healthy
She is safe
We are strong.

seesaw

I am fine
I can't do this, again
I will get through
I am giving up
Positive thinking
I hate it
I fight for my children
My fight is drained
I'll feel better tomorrow
Every day hurts
I have support
Leave me alone
Everyone says I look great
Half my hair is gone
I look forward to traveling
I may not make it to next year

I am fine

keep crawling

The desert is dry. I must get to you. I pull
my leg one more step. And then the other.
I have to keep going. My last drop of water
drank long ago, my skin dry leather cracking
open. The air, sandpaper against it. I must
keep going. I can hear your voice in the wind.
I can see you in the distance. Just as I think

I am about to touch you... I reach out to feel
you, but I am still too far. Someone keeps
moving you just out of my reach. One more
step I tell myself. One knee drops to the ground.
No, get up, you're almost there. You told her
you would always be here for her, that you would
wait for her. Get up! Keep going. But my other leg

drops and my whole body gives in. My face falls
into the dry desert sand. I hear you again,
your little innocent voice, "Get up" you tell me,
Get up! Don't quit, You are almost here! I am waiting
for you! My heart starts beating faster. I stand
and try to run but can only walk. It's enough

to get to you, I think. I reach for you again
but my hand drops to the sand. I lose my strength,
falling on both knees and weep. A hoarse sob
as I have cried more tears than my body will make.
There are no tears left to fall. I am crawling now,

seeing you in the distance. All that I have lost.
All of you. All my descendants, with others who take
our places. The others that try to make you think
we are bad. You remember us, so you know better

but keep your feelings deep down so as to not ruffle
the feathers of those around you. You look over
your shoulder, discreetly so the others don't see

and you tell me to keep going, that you are counting
on me. And so I keep

c r a w l i n g.

BY JENNIFER BRYANT

I still hide
my journal.
Who am I
hiding it
from?

A ritual started
in fear:
re-reading
my own
thoughts,
not fear
of another's
discovery

Words recorded
in rice paper
notebooks.
Words that
perhaps
one day
could emerge
my next book,
or life lessons
when I am far
enough away
from them
to not feel
the sting
of shame.

I still hide
my journal.
As if these
feelings
could ever
really be
hidden.

hidden words

BY MELANIE SUE HICKS

perspective

At the light, you reached your hand
across the car to mine. I saw us

in your eyes, saw that most of our battles
only existed in my mind. Our differences,

judgments, and distances, you had not
made them. They were all mine. Your eyes

told me you were there all along, willing
and open. Feelings unspoken can mutate,

become cancerous. Your eyes said, I'm here.
Let's share. Tell me. Just tell me. We are Us.

And together, Us went onward.

BY LEE TYRELL BARRON

Monsoon season runs late in Nepal this year
I am drenched.
in every sense of the word
by the rain that soaks my clothes and hair
runs down my face

by the tsunami of voices
taunting me with
shame and condemnation and guilt
all muddled into one

You fucked it all up
too selfish, too bold

You fucked it all up
This life you had
his sadness
all your fault

The woman in the mirror
covered in mud and rain
In her eyes
I see love and perseverance
So what? So what if I fucked it all up?
Sometimes you have to wave goodbye
to those who can only love
who they want you to be
not who you are

I fucked it all up
I question,
or is my life
now right on track

I fucked it all up
or did he
perhaps this
fucked up
life is the right
life

Monsoon
season runs late
in Nepal
this year
I am drenched.
in every sense of the word
By the rain that soaks my
clothes and hair
runs down my face
By the tsunami of voices
Restoring me with
strength and
courage and
hope

all muddled
into one

talking back
to the voices

BY MELANIE SUE HICKS

uncontainable

I used to believe
I could carry
Or should, maybe carry
all the pain and heartache and suffering
by opening my arms
to absorb it all
into the massive ocean inside me
that taught the fish to swim
My penance for breadcrumbs
The ocean, I thought, was me
That it was me carrying it
in my lungs and legs
Trudging along the ocean floor
Mud and murk
The weight of the sun
pressing down on my head
pushing it under
It burned and made my neck ache and bones crumble
A thousand-pound weighted blanket
I'm aware it doesn't make a bit of fucking sense
But it is what I thought I was supposed to do
That I had to carry it all
For fear of ever releasing it
If I ever did let it go
It would swallow up everything
good and beautiful and right
I was the appointed container, after all
That was before I knew
I was no one's fucking container and much like the ocean
Could never actually be contained
So, I let go and no one died
Well, they did die

Both of them, less than a year apart
Somehow knowing, all my fault
Though I tried
To hold it all
The Puertoricanness
Not buried deep enough
in the sea of my
"I'm sorry I'm not
white enough,
narrow enough,
smooth enough,
petite enough
Bullet Rye whiskey
for medicinal purposes only,
of course, swallowed and gulped
The only tears he shared with me,
only me
Marines don't cry
That is, until the sky falls
in one hard sheet of cement
Then they take cover in fox holes
That was before I knew
I didn't have to swallow it all
Absorb it all, bear it all,
holding my breath
A thousand pounds of heat and pain
I didn't and I don't
I will never again
be contained or hold my breath
I do not carry the ocean
I glide through it with my iridescent scales
What I thought were cracks are gills
so now I breathe and float
Beloved, peaceful, and free

elephant

When we are born, we are not alone
There is an elephant in the room
Is the baby breathing?
Careful you don't choke
Don't fall down the stairs
Don't run into the street
Wear your coat
You'll catch your death of cold
Buckle up!
Drive safely!
Be careful
I love you
Please don't die

You will of course die
But someday, not today
Not until you are so old that the only thing you can see is the elephant
And the elephant carries you gently away
Please don't die before then

BY LEE TYRELL BARRON

dearest 11

Dearest 11-year-old me,
I wish I could meet your eyes that day
I don't remember all of it exactly
I know I slept on big plastic curlers
    making my head sore
To look smooth and soft and pretty
        I noted
I must not be any of those things
    naturally
I wore a starched white blouse
stiff and scratchy
buttoned all the way up
except not by me
    might make a mess
again,
        n o t e d
Pink corduroy skirt
I hated
because it pinched my waist
    but was
        the size
I should
    be
        after
all
        n o t e d
red puffy worm of an equator belt
        wrapped around me later
    maybe why I still hate pink

Definitely do not smile too wide

expose the gap and big teeth

   wouldn't want that

Now pinch your nose to

       t r a i n

       y o u r

       n o s t r i l s

       t r a i n

       t h e m

not to FLARE so big

       SO BIG

             SO

                        BIG

(which will sometimes echo forever)

       do

       not

       breathe

Sit tall

With your smooth and soft hair

tiny waist

modest smile

dainty nose

       hold

       S T I L L

Hold it

       A L L

           so very still

• • •

. . .

I wish I could meet your eyes that day
Speak through our single solo left cheek dimple
   Our own walkie-talkie wink
In a language you have not yet learned
   But somehow
      rings familiar
I would smiiiiiiiile
so big you'd see
      my great big teeth
less crooked now and slightly better fit
the full face that grew around them
I would make you giggle and catch the twinkle in your eye
   matching mine
I would fidget with the backdrop
Same stupid boring blue backdrop
   whisper in your ear
     that
     one
     day
Mija, you will jump into a fucking a waterfall and scrape your knee
climbing out
you won't even care
because you DID IT

exhilaration and radical JOY will overcome you
someone will take your picture
    at
    your
    request
Every bit of your glorious 47 year old body
  full and wide
    just like your smile
there are more dimples now and a hell of a lot more delight
    most days anyway
Memento of you and the journey
becoming and becoming and becoming
Turns out that just keeps happening, sweet girl
You will learn and keep learning
you were never going to be the doll your Mama
    thought she wanted
a tender parting gift of
       d e m e n t i a
will be her realization
neither
was
she
You'll share this brutiful lesson with her
Your Mama
redemption and healing with the little girl she thought she
abandoned in Vieques

•
:
•

but who came back out to play
from behind her
when her mind began to pull her away
before though
she
would
heal
through you
beloved mariposa
YOU
will help her   h e a l
Both these little girls would hold hands
     and each other
laugh so hard and silly and never ever try to hold it all or
still
     rarely giving their teeth,
wide and a little crooked and missing, even
     a second thought
giggling curls
spinning and twirling from both their heads
salt and pepper
        and   tea and honey
their bodies and laughter taking up
  so   much   more   space   and   magic

you will learn your light came from her fire
and you will learn to
b r e a t h e
and that
nothing about you
   or your Mama
was ever meant
to be
stiff
scratchy
pinching
dainty
tiny
and certainly not
still
or
the
least
bit
tame

BY FAITH SCOTT

origin

I am from creek beds, from cornfields,
coke plants, and sycamore trees along
the Wabash River. I am from race cars

and basketball, from dirty small towns
and white snow drifts to my chin. I am from
tulip bulbs and dogwood trees. I am from old
elevators in department stores, from Kingdom

Halls and Methodist pews, from newspaper
articles taped to walls, pulling yourself up
from bootstraps, and "never ever quits."

I'm from Saturday morning donuts and Scooby
Doo, from Glenn Miller and Dean Martin, from Mary
Tyler Moore, Kojak, and Carol Burnett, rabbit-eared
TVs and afghans on the davenport. I am from teenaged

uncles who die at 16 and at 19. I'm from grandmothers
crying in hospital hallways, from marriages spent
in separate bedrooms when a son is lost. I'm from Bob

and Pauline. I'm from Gene and Mary. I am from canned
salmon and trailer parks, mothers who leave and fathers
who stay. I am from Sally. I am from Steve. I am from
temporary families with step-brothers and kickball

in empty corner lots, Happy Days and Fantasy Island,
summer trips in a '77 Grand Prix, plush bench seats
and dusty windows, the three of us: Jason, Eric, and Krissy,

Oklahoma, Texas, Grand Canyon, Rocky Mountains.
I am from second-chance two-story houses and family
Christmas Eves. I'm from women who wanted to raise
me as their own. Diana. Janie. I'm from voices screaming,

doors slamming, and papers filed. I am from new beginnings,
old grudges. I am from cardboard boxes packed and curtains
hung in new apartments. I am from resilience created

out of chaos, from Winter to Summer and back, the first
yellow flower in Spring erupting from concrete.

BY KRIS LINGENFELTER

divorce in four acts

I.
All the men in my life are pointing
at me
and saying,
"This was your choice,"
as though they had nothing
to do
with any of it.

II.
Yes, I am drinking alone
at midnight.

But my son is asleep,
and he knows that he is safe

and loved.

III.
Some days, you will involuntarily recall every
excruciating
detail
of this entire experience.

And each snippet of memory will break you
all
over
again.

You will feel the marrow leaking from your bones
as your tears melt the flesh from your cheeks.

You will lie to yourself and say
that at least -
at last -
it is finally over.

IV.
My reflection looks me directly in the eye,
unflinching,
though I try to turn away.

"This was your choice,"
she says,
lip curling into a wry smile.

"One day you'll stop lying
to yourself.

And then,

you'll begin again."

BY ERIN GALLEGOS

year of the fire

There are certain tree
seeds that can only crack
open in the blazing hot temperatures
of a wildfire. After the fire has passed,
new growth can take deep roots, becoming
strong and lush and vibrant, but the fire does
have to burn first. For me, this was the year of the
fire. The blaze that came through and is in some ways
still smoldering didn't reduce my joy to ash, but broke me
wide open and re-rooted my past even more securely within me.

BY SARAH HANSON

war cry

BY LEE TYRELL BARRON

A Prayer to My Body

Hello body, deep inside.
    Can you hear me, cells?

You have a job to do
    Rally up all the soldiers

    We have some cells to neutralize
    That's military speak for seek
        and destroy

These cells are trying to kill us,
and It's kill or be killed, so move fast
    Be the first to strike

Victory is the only option
Because death is the alternative

    These chemicals I pour in are to help you
    But they also can hurt you.

War is hell, cancer is a cliché,
I'm so over it.

    Please body,
        just win this war.

SHAKING OFF THE ASHES

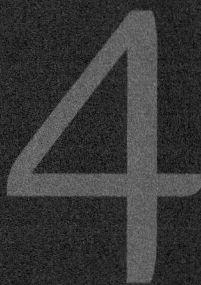

the view from above

POEMS OF RESURRECTION AND LIVING FREE

who i say i am

A mantra that rings bells in my soul: *May I have*
the courage to be who I say I am. Twelve simple
words. Rearview glances illuminate those times

> my courage has waned, when shiny objects
> and selfishness led to paths far distant from my ideal.
> Where I donned masks to cover shame, carried prisms

to distort the light away from truth, filling novels
with rationalizations, covering mirrors as to never look
myself in the eye. How heavy the bag of tools one must carry

> when keeping up appearances. Tonight, in the lavender fields
> I lay down that bag for good and replace it with a promise.
> May I have the courage to be who I say I am. I am a writer,

so I write. I am a storyteller, so I tell. I am an adventurer,
so I travel. I value nourishment, so I cook. I value work,
so I am productive. I value time, so I prioritize. I value service,

> so I give back. I value truth, so I speak truth. I value authenticity,
> so I hold no secrets. I value peace, so I draw boundaries.
> I value loved ones, so I show up. I value love, so I do love.

May I have the courage to be who I say I am. This does not
mean perfection, the utopian fallacy, but rather owning mistakes
without shame or hiding, growing so as to not repeat.

> This does not mean falling in line to fit societal whims.
> This does not mean loving others less if they differ
> in choices, but avoiding being drawn astray to their paths.

May I have the courage to be who I say I am.
Nothing more, nothing less, everyday for the rest of my life.

BY MELANIE SUE HICKS

remnants

I plunge my hands
into the deadwood of my past
again and again,

determined to reclaim
every remnant of my own goodness
felled before its time.

I am not leaving myself behind.

BY SARAH HANSON

freckles

A few freckles
Across a ski-slope nose
Smooth skin sliding to
Lips parted as you sleep
Safely in your parents' bed
Dreams of a nine-year-old boy

you have a grace

You have a grace

and elegance that creeps into my day.

Like a surreptitious hug from my deepest psyche.

How do you know I like that color?

How would you know I love that font,

that brush, that song or sound?

Where does your sense of style come from

that oozes into mine?

It holds me captive

like a moment in your eyes.

BY MAURA McLAUGHLIN

ornaments of the soul

We sat on his couch, among boxes of Santa
statues, nutcrackers and garland. November,
but celebration has no timeline. I lamented:
my home may remain bare of décor after a year
dulled by pain.

Decorate anyway.

Fears race at the thought of unwrapping
memories papered as ornaments. Bracelets
worn during his deployment. Painted gourds
from Sante Fe. Moroccan leather from our honeymoon.

Decorate anyway.

Tucked into grey tuffs, conversation flowing
down a mountain-fed waterfall, cascading
from childhood chapters of Disney joy
to disenchanted pain of adult betrayal.

Decorate anyway.

So different our lives, his lights and glitter
and fame. A larger-than-life spirit illuminating
the room. My quiet flame flickering the corner,
growing to a small fire on the rare moments
someone turned to notice my light.

Decorate anyway.

In the crevasse of our souls, shared parallels
emerge. Solace. Sacred space of home, calm
from the storm. Impulsivity. Changed flights,
gummy bears, a belief that life is a limited
collection of moments.

Affliction. How much of ourselves are we allowed
to show in this world? Do we armor up, head high,
plow through the warring factions? Wear earplugs
and blinders to the hate of those who oppose?
Or do we build pillow forts of comfort, burrowing
amid warm blankets that hide our luminosity?

Decorate anyway.

I dance in my dreams with a spotlight
finding my words. His floodlight amplifies
the burden of vulnerability. He thrives.
Would I trade him? Would I even survive?

Decorate anyway.

My home now glitters with red and green,
silver and gold. His words still echoing.
I have survived, and I decorate anyway.

BY MELANIE SUE HICKS

you will like it

BY MAURA McLAUGHLIN

over here

What do I do when my love is making art,
doing his thing,
taking his time?
I feed him.

What does he do when I'm engrossed
in my process?
He feeds me.

What do we do when we are both in our worlds
creating from our deep within?
We order take out.

That is all there is to do.
The only argument becomes
who's gonna call in the order!

linger

On Learning to Write A Love Poem to Myself and Believe It

Rest, Beloved

Then, rest some more

Linger, even

Delight in the breeze kissing the entirety of your gloriousness

Surrender to the passion of sunlight adoring you

Float your siren form majestic

In clearest blue cool

Rub bellies with Love

Gazing above where swallows swirl through clouds

Murmuration caressing every bit of your magnificence

Where no shadow could dare tread

BY FAITH SCOTT

sunflowers

Tiny hands around the stems,
a child's big smile cannot be dimmed,
for countless moments of my life
sunflowers were there.

And then in his hand at my front door,
the sight made my heartstrings sing.
I swore he was the only one
until the night he said goodbye.

Pain and tears, broken remnants
of my soul, petals strewn out on the floor.

See them now, I turn away
yellow, brown and words unsaid,
anger at the loss of him.
Life without them cold and stale.

Found again in far off fields
near a mountain where I healed
facing up toward the sun,
soul alive again.

Now I buy them for myself,
taking back their yellow joy.

BY MELANIE SUE HICKS

we got you lee

The moment we receive from others

A gift of support or items to cheer us

The urge, oh the urge to feel we have not given enough

To start thinking what we can do to give back, to make it even

To become a better person who does the giving

This is not the time to be better at giving

It is the time to be better at receiving

To receive with gratitude that is not tied to guilt

There can be time later to make choices to give

Not because we feel we should, but because the moment was
for giving

When a group of moms that I have known since my daughter
started kindergarten

Gave to me and said, 'We got you Lee'

I felt this inadequacy of receiving without giving back

Though I have known each of these individuals for years, we
are not close

We do not schedule time together

We know each other from casual conversations around the
school grounds

Or maybe at the supermarket

It was so hard to receive so much giving and to simply say

Thank you thank you thank you

Beyond what they tangibly give to me, they have given me

The gift of receiving with gratitude

And if and when I am able, I will pass it along

BY LEE TYRELL BARRON

on my 100th birthday

The things we would say when the hourglass
is slowly trickling its last sands, let me say
them now. Why wait to utter the words
that matter most. On my 100th birthday, let me

stand on a wooden bench and scream them out loud,
despite looks that scream fear of falling.
Because I am my mother's daughter, and also
I have fallen far too often to care any more.

On my 100th birthday, I raise a glass
of gratitude to my parents, who loved despite
never understanding me, from whom I grew
wings of my own and soft place to land.

On my 100th birthday I raise a glass
of gratitude to my lovers, some great and some shit.
Because of you, my depth of independence
grew. And also, my vulnerability and strength.

On my 100th birthday I raise a glass
of gratitude to my service organizations, who own
part of my soul and all of my heart in service to others,
And made me a better person in the process.

On my 100th birthday I raise a glass
of gratitude to the warrior women who loved
me. Because you held me, lifted me, honored me,
I thrived. And also, with humility I fall at your feet.

On my 100th birthday I leave with one
request. For anyone listening, when I leave
this earth, because I have no heirs
and also, long to be remembered:

On my 100th birthday, tell them I had a beautiful
soul, so they know I tried to be good to the world.
On my 100th birthday, tell them I was just a little bit
mean. So they know I was not perfect.

On my 100th birthday, tell them I showed
up, so they know my love of others
On my 100th birthday, simply tell them I *existed.*
Because that will be enough.

BY MELANIE SUE HICKS

BY SARAH HANSON

on my tombstone

On my tombstone I want it said:
This woman searched for truth.

She chased truth with both hands
open and fumbling and reaching.

She ached with her whole heart
to see and be seen as she was,

to connect past with present,
heart to art, soul to what is unchanging,

to be changed and seen and believed.
To be believed. To be believed.

i want what i want

The space of *want* held too big a spot for anyone to get to me.

When I put it there it keeps me from just knowing people as people.

I know I'm attracted to you all, it's a part of how I roll.

But the *want* I burst in exchange for my freedom of friendship and communion.

Let's have lunch instead.

BY MAURA McLAUGHLIN

morning hope

Hummingbird vigilant on the peach tree
branch, the size of a leaf. I have to focus
to know it's you watching over your kingdom.
Blue jays, a couple, noisily explore the seed

feeder, which is actually a flower pot hanging
on the fence. Those that I call little black-capped
chickadees have their turn. I watch you from
my table. Every morning I need to know you are

there, again and again. Your permanence
gives me comfort, hope. I might be here tomorrow
if you are. I might survive this winter, this year.
I replenish the seed to make sure you will come,

afraid you'll find a new source if I lag. Seeds drop
to the ground like sand in an hourglass. I watch
you and count the days I have gained.
Each time I sit down with my plate, there is a moment

before I look up, where I think you may not
be there. But you never fail me.

BY LEE TYRELL BARRON

you

I can do it alone
I know how
But I'd like to do it with
you
I can go there solo and
often do
But I'd like to go there
with you
I can live by myself it's
easy enough
But I'd like to wake up
with you
I can keep this a secret
and usually do .
But I'd like to share it
with you.

BY MAURA McLAUGHLIN

thirty-eight items

A tin shack, perfectly organized
in a mountain-side village in Nepal.
Table serves as pantry, every item
carefully in its place. Nails on the wall
for things to be removed and placed
back precisely as before.

A two burner table stove
powered by large propane tank,
four large water containers
and a pitcher to draw from them.
Everything made of stainless
steel except the four dal mini
goblets made of gold.

Four tea cups, four tall cups.
Four plates. A dozen bowls
of varying sizes. Two pots.
One knife. One ladle.
One vegetable peeler.

No refrigeration. No running
water. Nothing unused.
Nothing extra. Simple. Perfection.

In this kitchen, I learned
to make Nepalese food.
In this kitchen, I learned
true farm to table.
In this kitchen, I learned
what human connection is.
In this kitchen, I learned
the meaning of life.
In this kitchen, I learned
the meaning of love.

BY MELANIE SUE HICKS

wild things

You are outside, from my perspective. In the chilly
morning I am in my bathrobe, comfortable in the perfect
ambient temperature, holding my cup of coffee
with two hands You are eating the mixed seeds
I bought in a twenty-pound bag at Walmart. I think of you
as mine. My bird, in my yard. And though I have made
foraging a little easier for you, you are not mine.
You are wild. You belong to the chilly morning.
You have to find shelter when it rains and the winds
blow. You might die if you do not keep a keen eye out
for danger while you eat. You do not sit inside a sixty-four
degree room, safe from all the wild that lives outside,
watching through a glass door.

BY LEE TYRELL BARRON

isn't it obvious

I avoid you silly because I think you're cute.
I avoid you because one move and I'm in.
I avoid you because you will bring some fun.
I avoid you because you may not like me.
I avoid you because of others from my past.
I avoid you because I am waiting for you to jump.
What if you're avoiding me, too?

BY MAURA McLAUGHLIN

wilder

In the quiet aftermath of shattered dreams
life's fragility laid bare.
Charmed until tragic.
Reality an aberration.
A soundless howl
Or   gasping   for   air.
My back hits the wall.
Looping phone cord stretched taut.
Sliding to the floor is real
when the unreal, unimaginable occurs.
Nursing a soul ten days arrived
communicating with another just departed.
Grief the unwelcome guest
an empty chair
an absent smile.
Resilient and unwavering
love persists.
An enduring presence
imprinted on the living.
Strength and wisdom tragedy's scars.
Be Love, a silent psalm.
Live Forgiveness, echoed in each breath.
You always have a choice, she whispers,
When you are alive.

BY DEBORAH CAMPBELL

dance with me

On the occasion of my hundredth birthday,
I would tell you about my life.
But an old woman doesn't need to speak
of her past.
She simply contains it,
like wine in a raised glass.

It is in every line on her calloused hands,
nestling in the deep crevices of her cheeks,
clinging to the stubborn scars on her ancient knees,
Settled into the bruises dotting her thinning skin.

It resides in every pore, in every wrinkle of her sun-kissed face,
in every chamber of her beating heart,
in the breath that wheezes from her lungs
when she laughs.
Evidence of every minute she has spent loving,
losing, and living.

And so I will simply stand before you
with my glass raised,
and remind you to dance on my grave
when I'm gone.

I've ordered my tombstone already.

Dance with me.

a wednesday's prayer

TRUST - I was not being kind to you these last few days -
You and the universe are in sync - I forgot.

GRACE - so glad that you don't hold grudges when I forget to send
you out on my behalf.

LIFE - I was trying to slay you in my creative mind - I choose you now.

PEACE - be with you.

BY MAURA McLAUGHLIN

and beauty

grief

I'm so sad today, and.

And the sun is still warm,
and coffee still tastes good,
and our kitten
still wants infinite snuggles.

So, we drink our coffee
and read books
and snuggle the cat and each other
out in the morning sun.

Grief and beauty
don't cancel each other out;
they simply exist together.

I can feel my heart
and our house expanding
to hold even more complicated, hard,
beautiful, tender and true things

all at the same time.

BY SARAH HANSON

crib notes from the only ours

The story I have been telling myself
about myself
for too long
was actually everyone else's story of me
about me
the one that says
I solemnly hereby accept
responsibility
Such a big word for a baby
But never mind,
it was all my fault
and in so doing
until further notice
hold it all on my shoulders
tiny and rubbery bones
all the confusion
all the pain
all the struggle
the story that was already written
scribbled out and shoved between
the bars of my crib
a binding contract
notarized and sealed
saying I am hereby the container of all of it
the it that came before
Sealed in blood, even
Ok, technically, the blood came from paper cuts
Babies don't read the fine print
that stated things like
no questions

would ever be answered
rules needed to be followed
though never explained
just fall in line
Pay no mind to
numbers that do not add up
failing to do so means
never being worthy or good or loved or heard or known or held

Furthermore, you must accept the spin of spoiled
that is, to say, like milk
undeserving of nourishment
because after all
babies can't open screw top lids
The one that says when not in alignment with God
By which, that means what they defined as such
dark clouds will form
steaming brimstone
certainly not anointed
clearly doomed
there is a curse
black and heavy
like a tidal wave of turpentine
splashing, splattering like tar
coating, attacking, and stripping
stolen eggs and babies
stinging and scathing
such a shame she wouldn't fall in line
wide and stretched out
big as the roof of a house or parachute
impossible to hold with your hands by grabbing

• • •

your instinct to freeze
paralyzed and stunned
what a bizarre instinct
that's the story after all
since before I can remember
but somehow, should have already known
so foreign and heavy
weighted blanket of sand
wet and dark
sewn crudely along
the back of my wrists
up to my neck
the back at least
knotted tightly
spreading wide across my arms
like wings
dragging down
where I sink
only
ever
sink

until

something deeper in me
glowing and cool
balm of belovedness
begins to seep in
between the fiery sulfur fetters
loving liberation lifts
the tether of tainted tar
pulling me up to light and sky
reaching up and out
separating
lifting me
impossibly higher
rising toward the surface
warmest light
a new story
the truer one
a strangely
truthier truth revealed
slowly

. . .

-
-
-

each reach of the ocean tide on the shore
revealing more and more
glints of stained glass
Once shattered
now smooth and lovely
feeling impossible
still sometimes
except it wasn't
isn't
because here I am
each inch
each lean
each big heart-opening breath
I continue to feel the pulling apart
crude stitching
dissolving away
impossibly heavy glob
dropping away
soon, looking up
ahead
around
even behind
though I still feel the phantom pull
the scratches, cuts, tearing and stretching of my skin
I see more and more light
undeniable orange glow behind my eyelids
ever-present

along with more and more relief
I am releasing
trusting love, only love
more and more
no longer being crushed and wounded
at least not like before
when sinking beneath the big impossible glob
now I am releasing the pain from the wounds
from that old story
scrawled out and snuck in
crib notes from the only ours
dissolving like sea foam
everything is already in the already
"I'm dumping my pockets
in this new story"
steadying my wobbly legs on shore
letting go of all the rocks and shells
old withering receipts
opening my hands
letting go of the soggy faded remnants
admitting finally
I only want to be seen and heard and held
so now I dance with shore back and forth
joyful revolution of delight
"stars hold the dark by being light"
It's like you knew it before I did
or could
and so it is

BY FAITH SCOTT

beige

The enchanting Gravitational pull of the massive Ocean inside me has always held the Real me, the Essence of me, the Depth.

Historically, I would quietly slip away in plain sight, to dip in to visit, to feel, to be immersed, to be Free.

Only to resurface and return to the Beige, the predictable, the logical, the responsible, the respectable, the defendable, the dependable …

Because I thought that was what I was supposed to Do.

I used to believe in the desolate lack of choices, the incessant eternity of Beige, the unrelenting expectation of

"Fine", the thick weight of "Not Yet".

That was before I knew the pain of realizing I am the casualty of Indifference. Slowly paying with the non-refundable coins of my Life force and Dreams.

That was before I knew the Miracles engraved with my Name.

That was before I knew the Passion encoded in my Identity.

That was before I knew that Real Love was aching to find me too.

BY KIRBEE MILLER

about the curators

S A R A H   H A N S O N

An emerging poet with an MA from the University of Chicago, Sarah is currently finishing her first full-length collection of poems. Her work has been featured in Wild Greens, Prosectrics, and The Midnight Fawn Review. Sarah's writing explores such themes as: healing from abuse and trauma, creating meaningful connection, finding safety in authentic expression, and reintegrating with the natural world. The Minnesota native lives in downtown Minneapolis with her husband Jay, her three cats, and a codependent To Be Read book pile that will follow her into the afterlife.

MELANIE SUE HICKS

Speaker, Entrepreneur, Global Philanthropist. Traveling to 44 countries, she has spent two decades doing service work and studying human connection and resilience. She is the author of Incongruent; Travel, Trauma,  Transformation, a travel memoir from her journey to Everest Base Camp where she reflects on lessons of living amidst life's wreckage. Writing her first book at 10 years old, her work has been featured in popular magazines and websites including Forbes.com, Marie Claire, Authority Magazine, See Beyond Magazine, The District, Doctor's Life Magazine and Healthcare Business Digest. Born under Florida sunshine, she found her geographical soulmate in the Colorado Rocky Mountains where she enjoys hiking, biking, skiing, snowshoeing, and golf.

about the authors

DEB CAMPBELL

Crafted in the Midwest, seasoned in Texas, currently marinating in California. Eagerly anticipating what comes next!

ERIN GALLEGOS

Erin Penner Gallegos is a part-time poet, a sometime writer, and a fulltime overthinker. An American, Erin lives in Prague with her son, her partner Michal and his three children. Erin loves language and mountains and the sound of water making its way gently over smooth river stones; she loves travel, has a wicked but goofy sense of humor, and has cried in front of every boss she's had for the last 10 years. She's acquired enough life experience that some people mistake it for wisdom: call it Big Sister Energy, if you must. She loves a good strong cup of coffee, with milk, if you have it; otherwise, just black is fine. She's got a sixth sense for when someone needs a hug. Just beware, if you leave her alone in a house for long enough, she will find and consume all the chocolate.

Picture Credit Michal Trs.

FAITH SCOTT

Faith is a Licensed Professional Therapist, Writer, Trauma Informed Yogi, and Awkward-Brave-ish-Leaper. She has been in recovery since 1-23-22 and has been on a journey of radical healing, acceptance, and love. She laughs loud, cries often, and hugs (with consent) for ridiculously long stretches. Her writing is a kaleidoscope of reflections of all this through poetry and memoir.

JENNIFER FULTON BRYANT

Jennifer is a budding artist, green-thumb-gardening guru, and a hobby hopping junkie. She lives in Michigan with her husband.

KIRBEE MILLER

Kirbee launched her multi dimensional brand around the idea that communication in safe spaces is a powerful equalizer leading to beautiful conversation and connection. Taking her on a global journey and inspiring her guided cookbook + journal: NOURISH | A Guide to Coming Home to Yourself, Kirbee's road to entrepreneurship has not been without hardship. On New Year's Eve 2018, her parents were critically injured in a car accident, leaving Kirbee to spend many months sleeping in the hospital, advocating for her parents' care, and ultimately this experience has reinforced Kirbee's commitment to creating inclusive and meaningful moments that Nourish. Kirbee + Co.'s mission is to use voice and creativity to meaningfully cultivate connections.

KRIS LINGENFELTER

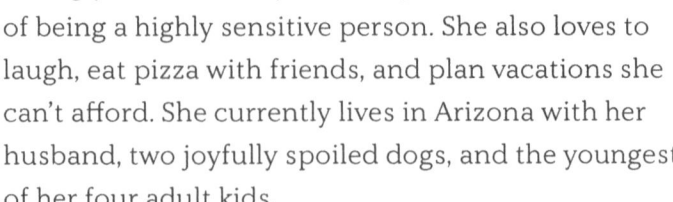

A restless writer and part-time mystic trapped in the body of a registered nurse, Kris loves to explore emotional connection through words and is strongly influenced by the complexities of being a highly sensitive person. She also loves to laugh, eat pizza with friends, and plan vacations she can't afford. She currently lives in Arizona with her husband, two joyfully spoiled dogs, and the youngest of her four adult kids.

LEE TYRELL BARRON

Lee enjoys writing and traveling with her husband and two children. She is a cancer fighter and often writes about her experiences and feelings related to this part of her life.

MAURA P. McLAUGHLIN

She writes from Maura's World: a perspective which travels from the firmament to the floor, feeling the pulse of the universe through her heart, rooted for years, in the city of Angels.

a note about neurodivergent women

While not all the authors in this work claim the distinction of neurodivergence as their own, the journey of this compilation has revealed a hidden secret many of us were holding within. Through the platform of our collected work, we seek to bring attention to the subject that so many, for decades, have discounted.

Attention-Deficit/Hyperactivity Disorder (ADHD) is the most commonly undiagnosed neurodivergent tendency in women today. While it is a condition that affects both men and women, research shows it is most often underdiagnosed or misdiagnosed in women.

Why Does This Matter?

Women with ADHD have higher rates of anxiety (35%-50%), depression (40%-60%), and eating disorders (especially binge eating and bulimia). We are also at a higher risk of developing substance use disorders compared to the general population. Hormonal changes throughout a woman's life, particularly during puberty, pregnancy, and menopause, can exacerbate ADHD symptoms.

Research indicates women with ADHD often experience lower educational attainment, frequent job changes, and lower self-esteem. We often report challenges in managing household tasks, maintaining relationships, and parenting, leading to increased stress and feelings of inadequacy.

The number of adult women diagnosed with ADHD has been increasing due to a growing awareness of how ADHD presents differently in women. This increase is actually a silver lining of sorts, as recognition is the first step to overcoming.

We Stand Together

The neurodivergent and neurotypical women in this book stand with those seeking to change the narrative. Many of us grew up hearing "you are too much", "it's all in your head", "it's not severe enough to matter", "it's just a label". All the while, we grew up not knowing that the gargantuan effort we were putting forth to survive life's obstacles was being amplified by our own disorder. Late-in-life diagnoses matter, as they help us overcome guilt and shame for the various ways we might have been ill-equipped to handle our emotional regulation, discombobulated behaviors, and extreme sensitivities.

The women in this book have embraced the notion put forth by leading scientists, writers and other celebrities including Dr. Patricia Quinn, Dr. Lidia Zylowska, Dr. Ellen Littman, Tracy Otsuka, Simone Biles, Ryan Gosling, Adam Levine, Richard Branson among others, that our ADHD and, for women, the coping skills we developed over years of misdiagnosis, are actually our super power.

Divergent thinking allows us to see connections that others might miss, which can lead to breakthroughs in problem-solving, art, and innovation. Our unusual hyperfocus helps to work with incredible efficiency, especially on complex or long-term projects. We can have high levels of energy and enthusiasm, which can be contagious and inspire others around us. Many thrive in entrepreneurial roles where we can harness creativity and risk-taking.

Individuals with ADHD often develop strong adaptability due to our need to navigate environments not designed for our brains. As a result, we can be highly resilient, finding new ways to cope with challenges or bounce back from setbacks.

Perhaps most important, ADHD women often have strong emotional intelligence and can be deeply empathetic, our heightened sensitivity helping to create meaningful relationships.

Like the relationships we, within these pages, developed in Tuscany. The ones that led us to open our souls in a way that bonded us for a lifetime. The ones that led us write the words found on these pages. Thank you for allowing us to share a glimpse into our human experience through the lens of poetry. May it inspire you, may it intrigue you, may it make you feel seen.

www.ingramcontent.com/pod-product-compliance
Lightning Source LLC
Chambersburg PA
CBHW050447150626
46551CB00029B/1975